MOTOCROSS

SPORTS CHALLENGE

DAVID ARMENTROUT

The Rourke Book Co., Inc.
Vero Beach, Florida 32964

David Armentrout specializes in nonfiction writing and has had several book series published for primary schools. He resides in Cincinnati with his wife and two children.

PHOTO CREDITS:
© Jamie Squire/Allsport: Cover, pages 7, 9, 16; © Dusty Willison/Intl Stock: pages 4, 10, 12, 13, 19, 21, 22; © G. E. Pakenham/Intl Stock: page 6; © Norris Clark/Intl Stock: pages 15, 18

EDITORIAL SERVICES:
Penworthy Learning Systems

Library of Congress Cataloging-in-Publication Data

Armentrout, David, 1962 -
    Motocross / by David Armentrout.
        p. cm. — (Sports challenge)
    Includes index.
    Summary: Presents basic information on the essential skills, techniques, and equipment for motocross.
        ISBN 1-55916-218-X
        1. Motocross—Juvenile literature. [1. Motocross.]
    I. Title II. Series: Armentrout, David, 1962 -   Sports challenge.
    GV1060.12.A76 1997
    796.7'56—dc21   97–12420
                                                              CIP
                                                              AC

Printed in the USA

TABLE OF CONTENTS

MOTOCROSS

Motocross (MO to KRAWS) is cross-country motorcycle racing—sometimes called off-road motorcycling. It is a fast-paced sport that takes riders through dirt and mud, up hills, around curves, and over bumps. It combines speed, power, and a whole lot of fun!

Motocross originated in Europe in the 1920's. Motorcycle riders wanted to challenge their abilities. They laid out a dirt race course and set out to prove they could control the two-wheeled machines on rough **terrain** (tuh RAYN). These races were called "scrambles."

A motocross rider gets airborne.

MOTOCROSS BIKES

Motocross bikes are classified by engine size, which is measured in cubic centimeters, or cc's. Most bikes are equipped with 125cc, 250cc, or 500cc engines. Riders select bikes that meet their riding abilities.

Riders choose bikes that fit their size and riding ability.

Motocross is a fast-paced sport.

The 125cc bikes are light and quick but wear easily. The 500cc bikes are bigger and heavier. They can reach high speeds in seconds but are hard to control on jumps and curves.

The 250cc bike combines the best of the 125cc and the 500cc bikes. It is a sturdy, lightweight bike that is easy to ride.

MOTOCROSS COMPETITION

Scrambles became known as motocross, or MX, at world championship events in the 1950's. International motocross riders compete at several levels, or classes. Riders as young as 7 years test their skill on bumpy dust-filled courses.

Most motocross riders are in their early teens. Riders begin to drop out of this physically and mentally demanding sport at about age fifteen. At this time the competition gets tough and the sport becomes more costly.

This rider competes on a 125cc bike.

CLOTHING AND SAFETY GEAR

Safety comes first in any action sport. A full-faced helmet is the most important piece of motocross gear. Only helmets certified by the Safety Helmet Council of America are allowed in competition. Goggles, padded gloves, motocross pants, and fitted leather boots are important too.

Body **armor** (AHR mur) reduces bumps and bruises. Unlike the medieval style, this armor is made of hard plastic and foam rubber that protects the shoulders, elbows, chest, and back if an accident should occur.

Body armor is worn for protection.

LEARNING THE SPORT

Where can you practice motocross? Motocross is noisy, and it can tear up the natural terrain. Therefore, you can practice in certain areas only.

The best way to learn how and where to motocross is to join a local club. A motocross bike dealer can help you find one.

Experienced motocross riders can help you learn the sport.

Practice in designated areas only.

Motocross clubs can help you get involved with others interested in the sport and tell you where you can ride. A club also keeps you informed of upcoming scrambles.

Preparing for a Race

One way to prepare for a race is to take a good look at the course before you ride. Walking the race course can help you figure out how to handle the curves and the straightaways.

Keep spare parts and tools on hand. You may need to do some minor bike repairs. Bring a change of clothes for after the race.

The best preparation is plenty of practice on motocross trails. You will get a feel for your bike while gaining confidence in your riding skills.

Motocross riders compete on bumpy, dust-filled race tracks.

TRIALS AND RACES

A standard motocross race is run on a course about one and a quarter miles long. The longest races are known as **enduros** (en DOOR oz). An enduro can take up to a week to complete and may cover hundreds of miles.

Riding skill—not speed—is most important in trials competition. In this contest, the riders compete with the terrain. The riders abilities are tested on rock, in mud, through forests, and sometimes across streams.

This rider keeps his weight back to skim over bumps at high speed.

RIDING THE BERM AND WHOOP-DE-DOOS

A banked wall of earth is called a **berm** (BERM). A berm is formed by the previous riders on the track. Riders choose the fastest line around the track— called the racing line—to ride around the berm. This technique is called berm bashing.

Racers scramble for the fastest line around the track.

Highly skilled riders are able to keep their bike steady on the high jumps.

Whoop-de-doos (HWOOP dee DOOZ) are closely spaced bumps. It is best to speed through them with bent knees and weight shifted back. This posture allows the bike to skim over the tops of the bumps.

BIKE CARE

Riding a motocross bike is tremendous fun, but it is important to take care of your bike. Keep a motocross bike clean. A garden hose can be used to wash away the mud after a race. Dry and polish the bike.

A set of tools can be costly, but learning to make a few adjustments yourself will save money in the long run. Follow an owner's manual to make routine checks of the engine fluids, tires, and other parts of the bike. Now you are ready for the next exciting day at the motocross races.

Motocross bikes have good suspension that absorbs shock on bumpy trails.

Glossary

armor (AHR mur) — protective clothing

berm (BERM) — a banked turn on a motocross course

enduros (en DOOR oz) — long races that test a riders endurance rather than speed

motocross (MO to KRAWS) — off-road motorcycle racing

terrain (tuh RAYN) — the surface of the ground

whoop-de-doos (HWOOP dee DOOZ) — closely spaced bumps on a motocross track

Motocross trails sometimes cross streams.

INDEX

GAYLORD M